AF228590

WHY DO CAMELS HAVE HUMPS?

by Debbie Vilardi

Cody Koala

An Imprint of Pop!
popbooksonline.com

abdobooks.com
Published by Pop!, a division of ABDO, PO Box 398166, Minneapolis, Minnesota 55439. Copyright © 2019 by POP, LLC. International copyrights reserved in all countries. No part of this book may be reproduced in any form without written permission from the publisher. Pop!™ is a trademark and logo of POP, LLC.

Printed in the United States of America, North Mankato, Minnesota

082018
012019

THIS BOOK CONTAINS RECYCLED MATERIALS

Cover Photo: iStockphoto
Interior Photos: iStockphoto, 1, 5 (top), 6–7, 9, 13, 17 (top), 17 (bottom left), 17 (bottom right), 18, 21; Shutterstock Images, 5 (bottom left), 5 (bottom right), 10 (bottom), 10 (top), 15; M. Watson/Science Source, 14

Editor: Meg Gaertner
Series Designer: Laura Mitchell

Library of Congress Control Number: 2018950145
Publisher's Cataloging-in-Publication Data
Names: Vilardi, Debbie, author.
Title: Why do camels have humps? / by Debbie Vilardi.
Description: Minneapolis, Minnesota : Pop!, 2019 | Series: Science questions | Includes online resources and index.
Identifiers: ISBN 9781532162176 (lib. bdg.) | ISBN 9781641855884 (pbk) | ISBN 9781532163234 (ebook)
Subjects: LCSH: Camels--Juvenile literature. | Dromedary--Juvenile literature. | Animals--Anatomy--Juvenile literature. | Children's questions and answers--Juvenile literature.
Classification: DDC 500--dc23

Hello! My name is

Cody Koala

Pop open this book and you'll find QR codes like this one, loaded with information, so you can learn even more!

Scan this code* and others like it while you read, or visit the website below to make this book pop.

popbooksonline.com/camels-have-humps

*Scanning QR codes requires a web-enabled smart device with a QR code reader app and a camera.

Table of Contents

Chapter 1

Adaptations

Many animals have **adaptations**. These are traits that help them live in certain **environments**.

Watch a video here!

Many camels live in the
desert. Deserts are very hot
and dry. There is little shade
from the sun.

Food is often hard to find.
Camels' humps help them
live in the desert.

Camels

There are two types of camels. The Bactrian camel has two humps on its back. The Arabian has one hump.

Learn more here!

Arabian
camel

Bactrian
camel

The humps store fat.
The fat is used for food
and **insulation**.

Food

A camel might not find food for weeks. It can still **survive** in the desert. It turns the fat stored in its hump into energy.

Learn more here!

The hump falls to one side. It gets smaller as the camel uses the fat.

When the camel eats

again, the hump fills up.

Insulation

Many animals store fat all over their bodies. This keeps them warm. But camels live in the hot desert. If camels did this, they would get too hot.

Complete an
activity here!

Camels' humps store extra fat. This keeps the rest of the camel's body cool during the day.

Camels do not sweat until it is more than 105 degrees Fahrenheit outside.

Deserts can get very cold at night. Camel humps store body heat during the day. At night, the heat spreads through the camel's body. The camel stays warm.

Making Connections

Text-to-Self

Have you ever seen a camel? What did you think of it?

Text-to-Text

Have you read other books about desert animals? How are they similar to or different from a camel?

Text-to-World

Since ancient times, people have used camels to cross the desert. Why do you think people use camels?

Glossary

adaptation – a trait that helps an animal survive in its environment.

desert – a dry area with little rainfall or plants.

environment – the natural world, including the land, sea, and air.

insulation – a material used to stop heat from passing through.

survive – to continue to live.

Index

Online Resources

popbooksonline.com

Thanks for reading this Cody Koala book!

Scan this code* and others like it in this book, or visit the website below to make this book pop!

popbooksonline.com/camels-have-humps

*Scanning QR codes requires a web-enabled smart device with a QR code reader app and a camera.